2018-2019 Teacher's Lesson Planner

This Planner Belongs To:

_____

36 Weeks of Hourly & Weekly Schedule
& Task Management for Students & Teachers

The School Year Ahead 2018-2019

July 2018

Su	Mo	Tu	We	Th	Fr	Sa
1	2	3	4	5	6	7
8	9	10	11	12	13	14
15	16	17	18	19	20	21
22	23	24	25	26	27	28
29	30	31				

August 2018

Su	Mo	Tu	We	Th	Fr	Sa
			1	2	3	4
5	6	7	8	9	10	11
12	13	14	15	16	17	18
19	20	21	22	23	24	25
26	27	28	29	30	31	

September 2018

Su	Mo	Tu	We	Th	Fr	Sa
						1
2	3	4	5	6	7	8
9	10	11	12	13	14	15
16	17	18	19	20	21	22
23	24	25	26	27	28	29
30						

October 2018

Su	Mo	Tu	We	Th	Fr	Sa
	1	2	3	4	5	6
7	8	9	10	11	12	13
14	15	16	17	18	19	20
21	22	23	24	25	26	27
28	29	30	31			

November 2018

Su	Mo	Tu	We	Th	Fr	Sa
				1	2	3
4	5	6	7	8	9	10
11	12	13	14	15	16	17
18	19	20	21	22	23	24
25	26	27	28	29	30	

December 2018

Su	Mo	Tu	We	Th	Fr	Sa
						1
2	3	4	5	6	7	8
9	10	11	12	13	14	15
16	17	18	19	20	21	22
23	24	25	26	27	28	29
30	31					

January 2019

Su	Mo	Tu	We	Th	Fr	Sa
		1	2	3	4	5
6	7	8	9	10	11	12
13	14	15	16	17	18	19
20	21	22	23	24	25	26
27	28	29	30	31		

February 2019

Su	Mo	Tu	We	Th	Fr	Sa
					1	2
3	4	5	6	7	8	9
10	11	12	13	14	15	16
17	18	19	20	21	22	23
24	25	26	27	28		

March 2019

Su	Mo	Tu	We	Th	Fr	Sa
					1	2
3	4	5	6	7	8	9
10	11	12	13	14	15	16
17	18	19	20	21	22	23
24	25	26	27	28	29	30
31						

April 2019

Su	Mo	Tu	We	Th	Fr	Sa
	1	2	3	4	5	6
7	8	9	10	11	12	13
14	15	16	17	18	19	20
21	22	23	24	25	26	27
28	29	30				

May 2019

Su	Mo	Tu	We	Th	Fr	Sa
			1	2	3	4
5	6	7	8	9	10	11
12	13	14	15	16	17	18
19	20	21	22	23	24	25
26	27	28	29	30	31	

June 2019

Su	Mo	Tu	We	Th	Fr	Sa
						1
2	3	4	5	6	7	8
9	10	11	12	13	14	15
16	17	18	19	20	21	22
23	24	25	26	27	28	29
30						

Federal Holidays 2018/19

Date	Holiday	Date	Holiday	Date	Holiday
Jul 4, 2018	Independence Day	Nov 12, 2018	Veterans Day (obs.)	Jan 1, 2019	New Year's Day
Sep 3, 2018	Labor Day	Nov 22, 2018	Thanksgiving Day	Jan 21, 2019	Martin L. King Day
Oct 8, 2018	Columbus Day	Dec 25, 2018	Christmas Day	Feb 18, 2019	Presidents' Day
Nov 11, 2018	Veterans Day			May 27, 2019	Memorial Day

This Week's Priorities

For the Week Of:

Top Priorities:

_____

Secondary Priorites:

1.)

2.)

3.)

_____

Things I can Push Into Next Week If I need to:

1.)

2.)

3.)

4.)

5.)

Lesson Plan

Subject	Monday	Tuesday	Wednesday

Week of: _____ to _____

Thursday	Friday	Notes

Recap of the Week:

This Week's Priorities

For the Week Of:

_____

Top Priorities:

_____

Secondary Priorites:

1.)

2.)

3.)

_____

Things I can Push Into Next Week If I need to:

1.)

2.)

3.)

4.)

5.)

Lesson Plan

Subject	Monday	Tuesday	Wednesday

Week of: _____ to _____

Thursday	Friday	Notes

Recap of the Week:

This Week's Priorities

For the Week Of:

Top Priorities:

_____

Secondary Priorites:

1.)

2.)

3.)

_____

Things I can Push Into Next Week If I need to:

1.)

2.)

3.)

4.)

5.)

Lesson Plan

Subject	Monday	Tuesday	Wednesday

Week of: _____ to _____

Thursday	Friday	Notes

Recap of the Week:

This Week's Priorities

For the Week Of:

Top Priorities:

_____

Secondary Priorites:

1.)

2.)

3.)

_____

Things I can Push Into Next Week If I need to:

1.)

2.)

3.)

4.)

5.)

Lesson Plan

Subject	Monday	Tuesday	Wednesday

Week of: _____ to _____

Thursday	Friday	Notes

Recap of the Week:

This Week's Priorities

For the Week Of:
_____

Top Priorities:

_____

Secondary Priorites:

1.)

2.)

3.)

_____

Things I can Push Into Next Week If I need to:

1.)

2.)

3.)

4.)

5.)

Lesson Plan

Subject	Monday	Tuesday	Wednesday

Week of: _____ to _____

Thursday	Friday	Notes

Recap of the Week:

This Week's Priorities

For the Week Of:

_____

Top Priorities:

_____

Secondary Priorites:

1.)

2.)

3.)

_____

Things I can Push Into Next Week If I need to:

1.)

2.)

3.)

4.)

5.)

Lesson Plan

Subject	Monday	Tuesday	Wednesday

Week of: _____ to _____

Thursday	Friday	Notes

Recap of the Week:

This Week's Priorities

For the Week Of:

Top Priorities:

_____

Secondary Priorites:

1.)

2.)

3.)

_____

Things I can Push Into Next Week If I need to:

1.)

2.)

3.)

4.)

5.)

Lesson Plan

Subject	Monday	Tuesday	Wednesday

Week of: _____ to _____

Thursday	Friday	Notes

Recap of the Week:

This Week's Priorities

For the Week Of:
_____

Top Priorities:

_____

Secondary Priorites:

1.)

2.)

3.)

_____

Things I can Push Into Next Week If I need to:

1.)

2.)

3.)

4.)

5.)

Lesson Plan

Subject	Monday	Tuesday	Wednesday

Week of: _____ to _____

Thursday	Friday	Notes

Recap of the Week:

This Week's Priorities

For the Week Of:

_____

Top Priorities:

_____

Secondary Priorites:

1.)

2.)

3.)

_____

Things I can Push Into Next Week If I need to:

1.)

2.)

3.)

4.)

5.)

Lesson Plan

Subject	Monday	Tuesday	Wednesday

Week of: _____ to _____

Thursday	Friday	Notes

Recap of the Week:

This Week's Priorities

For the Week Of:
_____

Top Priorities:

_____

Secondary Priorites:

1.)

2.)

3.)

_____

Things I can Push Into Next Week If I need to:

1.)

2.)

3.)

4.)

5.)

Lesson Plan

Subject	Monday	Tuesday	Wednesday

Week of: _____ to _____

Thursday	Friday	Notes

Recap of the Week:

This Week's Priorities

For the Week Of:
_____

Top Priorities:

_____

Secondary Priorites:

1.)

2.)

3.)

_____

Things I can Push Into Next Week If I need to:

1.)

2.)

3.)

4.)

5.)

Lesson Plan

Subject	Monday	Tuesday	Wednesday

Week of: _____ to _____

Thursday	Friday	Notes

Recap of the Week:

This Week's Priorities

For the Week Of:

_____

Top Priorities:

_____

Secondary Priorites:

1.)

2.)

3.)

_____

Things I can Push Into Next Week If I need to:

1.)

2.)

3.)

4.)

5.)

Lesson Plan

Subject	Monday	Tuesday	Wednesday

Week of: _____ to _____

Thursday	Friday	Notes

Recap of the Week:

This Week's Priorities

For the Week Of:

Top Priorities:

Secondary Priorites:

1.)

2.)

3.)

Things I can Push Into Next Week If I need to:

1.)

2.)

3.)

4.)

5.)

Lesson Plan

Subject	Monday	Tuesday	Wednesday

Week of: _____ to _____

Thursday	Friday	Notes

Recap of the Week:

This Week's Priorities

For the Week Of:

Top Priorities:

Secondary Priorites:

1.)

2.)

3.)

Things I can Push Into Next Week If I need to:

1.)

2.)

3.)

4.)

5.)

Lesson Plan

Subject	Monday	Tuesday	Wednesday

Week of: _____ to _____

Thursday	Friday	Notes

Recap of the Week:

This Week's Priorities

For the Week Of:
_____

Top Priorities:

_____

Secondary Priorites:

1.)

2.)

3.)

_____

Things I can Push Into Next Week If I need to:

1.)

2.)

3.)

4.)

5.)

Lesson Plan

Subject	Monday	Tuesday	Wednesday

Week of: _____ to _____

Thursday	Friday	Notes

Recap of the Week:

This Week's Priorities

For the Week Of:
_____

Top Priorities:

_____

Secondary Priorites:

1.)

2.)

3.)

_____

Things I can Push Into Next Week If I need to:

1.)

2.)

3.)

4.)

5.)

Lesson Plan

Subject	Monday	Tuesday	Wednesday

Week of: _____ *to* _____

Thursday	Friday	Notes

Recap of the Week:

This Week's Priorities

For the Week Of:

Top Priorities:

Secondary Priorites:

1.)

2.)

3.)

Things I can Push Into Next Week If I need to:

1.)

2.)

3.)

4.)

5.)

Lesson Plan

Subject	Monday	Tuesday	Wednesday

Week of: _____ to _____

Thursday	Friday	Notes

Recap of the Week:

This Week's Priorities

For the Week Of:
_____

Top Priorities:

_____

Secondary Priorites:

1.)

2.)

3.)

_____

Things I can Push Into Next Week If I need to:

1.)

2.)

3.)

4.)

5.)

Lesson Plan

Subject	Monday	Tuesday	Wednesday

Week of: _____ to _____

Thursday	Friday	Notes

Recap of the Week:

This Week's Priorities

For the Week Of:
_____

Top Priorities:

_____

Secondary Priorites:

1.)

2.)

3.)

_____

Things I can Push Into Next Week If I need to:

1.)

2.)

3.)

4.)

5.)

Lesson Plan

Subject	Monday	Tuesday	Wednesday

Thursday	Friday	Notes

Recap of the Week:

This Week's Priorities

For the Week Of:

Top Priorities:

Secondary Priorites:

1.)

2.)

3.)

Things I can Push Into Next Week If I need to:

1.)

2.)

3.)

4.)

5.)

Lesson Plan

Subject	Monday	Tuesday	Wednesday

Week of: _____ *to* _____

Thursday	Friday	Notes

Recap of the Week:

This Week's Priorities

For the Week Of:

Top Priorities:

_____

Secondary Priorites:

1.)

2.)

3.)

_____

Things I can Push Into Next Week If I need to:

1.)

2.)

3.)

4.)

5.)

Lesson Plan

Subject	Monday	Tuesday	Wednesday

Week of: _____ to _____

Thursday	Friday	Notes

Recap of the Week:

This Week's Priorities

For the Week Of:
_____

Top Priorities:

_____

Secondary Priorites:

1.)

2.)

3.)

_____

Things I can Push Into Next Week If I need to:

1.)

2.)

3.)

4.)

5.)

Lesson Plan

Subject	Monday	Tuesday	Wednesday

Week of: _____ to _____

Thursday	Friday	Notes

Recap of the Week:

This Week's Priorities

For the Week Of:

Top Priorities:

Secondary Priorites:

1.)

2.)

3.)

Things I can Push Into Next Week If I need to:

1.)

2.)

3.)

4.)

5.)

Lesson Plan

Subject	Monday	Tuesday	Wednesday

Week of: _____ to _____

Thursday	Friday	Notes

Recap of the Week:

This Week's Priorities

For the Week Of:

Top Priorities:

Secondary Priorites:

1.)

2.)

3.)

Things I can Push Into Next Week If I need to:

1.)

2.)

3.)

4.)

5.)

Lesson Plan

Subject	Monday	Tuesday	Wednesday

Week of: _____ to _____

Thursday	Friday	Notes

Recap of the Week:

This Week's Priorities

For the Week Of:
_____

Top Priorities:

_____

Secondary Priorites:

1.)

2.)

3.)

_____

Things I can Push Into Next Week If I need to:

1.)

2.)

3.)

4.)

5.)

Lesson Plan

Subject	Monday	Tuesday	Wednesday

Week of: _____ to _____

Thursday	Friday	Notes

Recap of the Week:

This Week's Priorities

For the Week Of:

Top Priorities:

Secondary Priorites:

1.)

2.)

3.)

Things I can Push Into Next Week If I need to:

1.)

2.)

3.)

4.)

5.)

Lesson Plan

Subject	Monday	Tuesday	Wednesday

Week of: _____ to _____

Thursday	Friday	Notes

Recap of the Week:

This Week's Priorities

For the Week Of:

_____

Top Priorities:

_____

Secondary Priorites:

1.)

2.)

3.)

_____

Things I can Push Into Next Week If I need to:

1.)

2.)

3.)

4.)

5.)

Lesson Plan

Subject	Monday	Tuesday	Wednesday

Week of: _____ to _____

Thursday	Friday	Notes

Recap of the Week:

This Week's Priorities

For the Week Of:

Top Priorities:

_____

Secondary Priorites:

1.)

2.)

3.)

_____

Things I can Push Into Next Week If I need to:

1.)

2.)

3.)

4.)

5.)

Lesson Plan

Subject	Monday	Tuesday	Wednesday

Week of: _____ to _____

Thursday	Friday	Notes

Recap of the Week:

This Week's Priorities

For the Week Of:

Top Priorities:

Secondary Priorites:

1.)

2.)

3.)

Things I can Push Into Next Week If I need to:

1.)

2.)

3.)

4.)

5.)

Lesson Plan

Subject	Monday	Tuesday	Wednesday

Week of: _____ *to* _____

Thursday	Friday	Notes

Recap of the Week:

This Week's Priorities

For the Week Of:

Top Priorities:

Secondary Priorites:

1.)

2.)

3.)

Things I can Push Into Next Week If I need to:

1.)

2.)

3.)

4.)

5.)

Lesson Plan

Subject	Monday	Tuesday	Wednesday

Week of: _____ to _____

Thursday	Friday	Notes

Recap of the Week:

This Week's Priorities

For the Week Of:

Top Priorities:

_____

Secondary Priorites:

1.)

2.)

3.)

_____

Things I can Push Into Next Week If I need to:

1.)

2.)

3.)

4.)

5.)

Lesson Plan

Subject	Monday	Tuesday	Wednesday

Week of: _____ to _____

Thursday	Friday	Notes

Thursday	Friday	Notes

Recap of the Week:

This Week's Priorities

For the Week Of:

Top Priorities:

Secondary Priorites:

1.)

2.)

3.)

Things I can Push Into Next Week If I need to:

1.)

2.)

3.)

4.)

5.)

Lesson Plan

Subject	Monday	Tuesday	Wednesday

Week of: _____ to _____

Thursday	Friday	Notes

Recap of the Week:

This Week's Priorities

For the Week Of:

_____

Top Priorities:

_____

Secondary Priorites:

1.)

2.)

3.)

_____

Things I can Push Into Next Week If I need to:

1.)

2.)

3.)

4.)

5.)

Lesson Plan

Subject	Monday	Tuesday	Wednesday

Week of: _____ to _____

Thursday	Friday	Notes

Recap of the Week: _____

This Week's Priorities

For the Week Of:
_____

Top Priorities:

_____

Secondary Priorites:

1.)

2.)

3.)

_____

Things I can Push Into Next Week If I need to:

1.)

2.)

3.)

4.)

5.)

Lesson Plan

Subject	Monday	Tuesday	Wednesday

Week of: _____ to _____

Thursday	Friday	Notes

Recap of the Week:

This Week's Priorities

For the Week Of:
_____

Top Priorities:

_____

Secondary Priorites:

1.)

2.)

3.)

_____

Things I can Push Into Next Week If I need to:

1.)

2.)

3.)

4.)

5.)

Lesson Plan

Subject	Monday	Tuesday	Wednesday

Week of: _____ to _____

Thursday	Friday	Notes

Recap of the Week:

This Week's Priorities

For the Week Of:

Top Priorities:

Secondary Priorites:

1.)

2.)

3.)

Things I can Push Into Next Week If I need to:

1.)

2.)

3.)

4.)

5.)

Lesson Plan

Subject	Monday	Tuesday	Wednesday

Week of: _____ to _____

Thursday	Friday	Notes

Recap of the Week:

This Week's Priorities

For the Week Of:
_____

Top Priorities:

_____

Secondary Priorites:

1.)

2.)

3.)

_____

Things I can Push Into Next Week If I need to:

1.)

2.)

3.)

4.)

5.)

Lesson Plan

Subject	Monday	Tuesday	Wednesday

Week of: _____ to _____

Thursday	Friday	Notes

Recap of the Week:

Recap of the Year

Thank You for using our Planner!
We appreciate your business!

If you liked this planner please return to where you purchased this one to chose your next planner from our latest collection.

Our brands are:
Renegade Notebooks & Smartly Bound

You will find our collection by searching for "Renegade Notebooks" or "Smartly Bound" at your favorite online bookseller.

RENEGADE NOTEBOOKS
NOTEBOOKS, JOURNALS, DIARIES & COMPOSITION BOOKS WITH ATTITUDE

SMARTLY BOUND
Notebooks, Journals & Composition Books

Made in the USA
Las Vegas, NV
04 March 2021